Sincerely Yours BIFF

CHRIS GARRATT and MICK KIDD

The following cartoons first appeared in the pages of
The Guardian and *City Limits* during 1985 and 1986.

SINCERELY YOURS

A CORGI BOOK 0 552 992542

First publication in Great Britain

PRINTING HISTORY
Corgi edition published 1986

Corgi Books are published by Transworld Publishers Ltd,
61–63 Uxbridge Road, Ealing, London W5 5SA, in Australia by
Transworld Publishers (Australia) Pty Ltd, 15–23 Helles
Avenue, Moorebank, NSW 2170, and in New Zealand by
Transworld Publishers (NZ) Ltd, Cnr Moselle and
Waipareira Avenues, Henderson, Auckland.

Made and printed in Great Britain by
Butler & Tanner Ltd, Frome and London

...AND ALL OUR YESTERDAYS...

HMM— SHALL I USE MY GREENPEACE DIARY HERE AND KEEP MY ASTROLOGICAL ONE FOR THE OFFICE..? (BRAIN SWITCHES INTO FLASHBACK MODE)

"THIS IS MY FIRST ENTRY OF A BRAND NEW YEAR. J.B. SMILED AT ME TODAY. SEEING HOOTER AND CHEESEY TONIGHT OUTSIDE PALAIS DE DANSE. WISH I COULD FRUG LIKE EVERYONE ELSE..."

FURY
EDEN KANE
SHANE FENTO
KARL DENVE
JACKY LINTON

TRAIN-SPOTTERS DIARY 1960

"..DYLAN SAYS IT ALL REALLY— PITY HE WENT ELECTRIC.."

TURN THAT INFERNAL RACKET DOWN!

"AN' THE CHAINS ERV THE SEA WILL UV BUSTED IN THE NIGHT, AN' BE BURIED AT THE BUDDUM ERV THE ERR-SHERN"

1965 DIARY

".GOT REALLY OUT OF IT LAST NIGHT AT THE ROUNDHOUSE. WOKE UP AFTER AMAZING DREAM BUT COULDN'T FIND PEN. STILL, AS HESSE SAYS, EVERY THOUGHT BELONGS TO ETERNITY EVEN THOUGH NO-ONE SEES OR HEARS IT..."

Grateful Dead

Whole Earth Diary 1969

let's get together

"....AS A MEMBER OF THE REVOLUTIONARY VANGUARD I SUPPOSE KEEPING A DIARY IS PRETTY INDIVIDUALISTIC. ON THE OTHER HAND, I MIGHT BE FAMOUS ONE DAY, AND SUCH CONTRADICTIONS OF PERSONALITY WILL GIVE MY BIOGRAPHERS SOMETHING TO CHEW OVER."

BIG RED DIARY 1973

"...TAKING ALL MY B.O.F. RECORDS AND PAPERBACKS DOWN TO JUMBLE SALE. NO MORE ENTRIES AFTER THIS..."

JOHNNY ROTTEN DIARY 1977

HEY DAD— WAKE UP! WAYNE AND I ARE OFF UP THE PUB. DO YOU WANT TO JOIN US?

HANG ON... ...I JUST HAVE TO FILL IN MY DIARY FOR JAN 1ST.

".....PHONE WASHING MACHINE REPAIR MAN..CAR FOR SERVICE AND M.O.T.... PHONE DEREK RE UPDATING '86 DESIGNS... PHOTOCOPY MINUTES OF EXEC. MEETING.. TAKE INTERVIEW SUIT TO CLEANERS... PHONE ANALYST..."

I STARTED THE YEAR BUOYANT WITH OPTIMISM..

I HAVE A POWER THAT NO MAN HAS EVER KNOWN...SOME KIND OF STRANGE MENTAL MUTATION! BY CONCENTRATION, WITH THE WISH IN MY MIND AND THE POWER THAT TRANSMITS TO MY EYES I CAN ENGAGE IN ALL MANNER OF CREATIVE PURSUITS!

GINO'S SOHO EATERIE OPEN TILL LATE.

REALLY? —I MUST HAVE YOUR PHONE NUMBER FOR MY FILOFAX.

3 BOTTLES OF VINO LATER I RETURNED TO MY PIED-A-TERRE...

RIGHT! NO SHILLY-SHALLYING!.. STRAIGHT DOWN TO WORK!

48

YOUR DAD PHONED.

THE SPECIAL FEATURES IN BILL'S ROOM ARE DESIGNER WALLPAPER, A HAIRDRYER AND A MOTH-EATEN DUVET...

BUT ERE LONG I WAS BACK TO MY BAD OLD WAYS-DWELLING ON SURFACE APPEARANCES,

I THINK IT STILL NEEDS A BIT OFF THE SIDES..

ABANDONING WORK ON THE SLIGHTEST PRETEXT..

TERRY'S GUESTS TONIGHT INCLUDE LIZA MINELLI AND MICHAEL HESELTINE..

HMM..

BC1

Chapter One. The s that n normal

AND FINALLY SLUMPING INTO LETHARGY.

...AND NOW, OVER TO PHILIP YET AGAIN FOR THE WEATHER PROSPECTS...

INTENSE SELF-CRITIQUE WORST CASE SCENARIO ETC...

WELL JOHN, ANOTHER GREY DAY IN STORE.... IN FACT, DON'T WORRY IF YOU THINK LIFE'S GONE FLAT.... SEASONAL AFFECTIVE DEPRESSION-S.A.D.-IS VERY COMMON AT THIS TIME OF YEAR...

BERDOING!

I ALLOWED A WAN SMILE TO PLAY UPON MY LIPS...

...IT'S TO DO WITH LACK OF SUNLIGHT! IN FACT, THE FINNS HAVE A REALLY HARD TIME OF IT IN JANUARY. SIBELIUS WENT TO THE CANARIES TO COMPOSE...

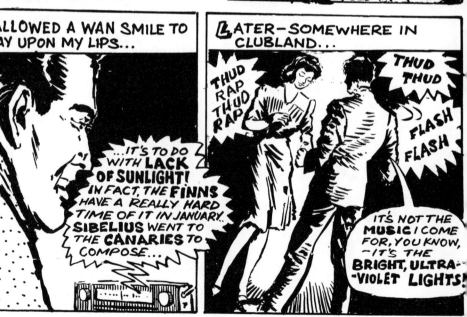

LATER-SOMEWHERE IN CLUBLAND...

THUD RAP THUD RAP

THUD THUD

FLASH FLASH

IT'S NOT THE MUSIC I COME FOR, YOU KNOW, —IT'S THE BRIGHT, ULTRA-VIOLET LIGHTS!

AT HOME

■ He tore stoically into a cheese and ham toastie, looked completely exhausted and talked for at least an hour and a half with energy, humour, gentleness and charm.

Artists talking about their work and making a few bob on the side. This week: TRISTAN BLAKE, writer.

"I'M USUALLY AT MY DESK BY 8·30 9·30 10·30 A.M.

WELL, THAT'S CLEANED THE OVEN, LOADED THE WASHING MACHINE, FED THE DOG AND DONE MY CANADIAN AIR FORCE EXERCISES — BETTER GET STUCK IN!

"SOME DAYS, EVERYTHING FALLS INTO PLACE..."

HOPEFULLY IT'LL BE A SPRAWLING PANORAMIC SAGA SPANNING THE DECADES...EARLY DAYS YET...

Sleet fell steadily on the small Kent town of Tunbridge Wells, just as weatherman Jack Scott had predicted, but for once, pensioner Mrs. Olive Penrose-Smith didn't notice the icy wind. Snugly settled in the depths of a luxury limousine with her live-in lover, Bill, she

CLATTER CLATTER DING CLATTER

"...WHILST ON OTHERS, IT'S AN UPHILL STRUGGLE."

SCHUBERT OF COURSE WAS ONLY 31 WHEN HE DIED, BUT IN FIFTEEN PRODUCTIVE YEARS LEFT OVER 1000 COMPLETED PIECES...

OKAY! OKAY, I KNOW! AND MOZART STARTED AGED 4...I'M A LATE DEVELOPER...BESIDES, THEY DIDN'T HAVE T.V. OR INSTANT COFFEE IN THOSE DAYS!

© 1986 BIFF PRODUCTS

"STILL, I'M PRIVELEGED TO BE ON MY OWN INNER JOURNEY I SUPPOSE..."

TEMPER! TEMPER! -IT'S ONLY YOURSELF YOU'RE HURTING!

YOU'VE CAUGHT ME ON A BAD DAY, READERS!

KERRANG!

SMASHING! CAN WE JUST DO A COUPLE OF RE-TAKES OF YOU FIXING THE TYPEWRITER, THEN WE'LL CALL IT A DAY...WHAT'S YOUR SCHEDULE FOR TOMORROW?

LET'S SEE...AT DESK 8·30 A.M...LUNCH WITH MAILER....

IS THIS A WRAP, KEVIN?

HERE LIFE IS DIFFERENT

THIS WEEK'S HEART-RENDING TALE ~ "I'm Glad You Called"

SORRY—NO **VALENTINES** AGAIN THIS YEAR... ..STILL, THE TAXMAN LOVES YOU, **ARF-ARF!**

OH WELL—I WON'T LET IT GET ME DOWN.. ..THERE'S PLENTY WORSE OFF THAN ME...

IT'S AWFUL HERE! DOUG AND MARIA AREN'T TALKING TO EACH OTHER, NO-ONE CLEANS THE STOVE ANY MORE AND DON IS LEARNING TO PLAY THE **BASS GUITAR**

KNOCK-KNOCK!

HOLD ON—THERE'S SOMEONE AT THE FRONT DOOR.

WELL, LISA—I HOPE YOUR RELATIONSHIP SURVIVES INTACT.... MAYBE YOU SHOULD **SOCIALISE** MORE.. —SORRY TO SOUND SO HARD...

NO—YOU'VE HELPED A LOT.. ..YOU'RE SUCH A **GOOD LISTENER.**

RING-RING!

...MY MIND IS LIKE A **THEATRE** THAT'S GONE **DARK**, TONY.... DO YOU THINK IT COULD BE **HALLEY'S COMET** —OR IS IT MY **PERSONALITY?**

KNOCK-KNOCK!

...SLEEP ON IT, SHOULD..IT'S A QUESTION OF REACHING **DECISION**...THINGS SHOULD FALL INTO PLACE AFTER THAT.

WELL, THANKS FOR LETTING THE **PERSON WITHIN** PEEP OUT A LITTLE...

LATER...

GOSH—I'M GLAD I I DON'T HAVE ALL THOSE **PROBLEMS!**

..BUT AM I BEING SMUG AND SELF-SATISFIED?

FLASH-FLASH

HANG ON—NOT **ONE** OF THEM ASKED HOW **I** WAS FEELING!

COMING NEXT—HOW **PRINCESS DIANA** RECEIVED A SPECIAL VALENTINE FROM LITTLE JASON TAYLOR WHEN SHE VISITED HIS CRECHE AT....

BAH! NOBODY CARES ABOUT ME!

ITN

BIFF PRODUCTS

How To Behave At A Preview.

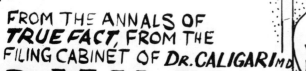

FROM THE ANNALS OF *TRUE FACT,* FROM THE FILING CABINET OF *Dr. CALIGARI* MD

PAY NOW, LIVE LATER

I'M A-GOIN' WHERE A MAN IS KNOWN BY HIS NAME, NOT HIS REPUTATION.

LET ME TELL YOU ABOUT MY FRIEND *GARY.* I'VE LAUGHED WITH GARY, I'VE CRIED WITH HIM—I'VE WRITTEN A BOOK ABOUT HIM...

DIAL-A-SHRINK
WHILE-U-WAIT ANALYSIS
PALMS READ
MORTGAGES ARRANGED

...GARY'S AN ABSOLUTELY *BEAUTIFUL HUMAN BEING.* THIS IS HIS STORY...

EARLIER THAT SAME DAY...

...AND THEN THIS BULLY NAMED LAWSON TOOK MY FOOTBALL AND PUNCTURED IT...

INSTITUTE OF HYPNOTISTS
Certificate

POT NOODL

—THERE'S ALWAYS A *LAWSON* IN LIFE, PAL.

~ GARY WAS ALWAYS TRYING TO BE POPULAR, EVEN IN THE **SCHOOLYARD**...

WHEN WE ARE MARRIED I'LL COOK US SAUSAGE FOR TEA, OKAY?

WHAT IF I'M *VEGETARIAN?*

HE FELT HE HAD TO APPEAR **STRONG** AND **CAPABLE** ON ALL OCCASIONS.

YOUTH CLUB NOTICES

ANIMA
DANCE

HMM! THIS MUST BE THE NEW *MACHO!*

GOSH ALICE...IF ALL I HAVE TO DO FOR YOU TO LIKE ME IS DROP A TEMPLE ON MY HEAD, I'LL DO IT EVERY WEEK!

..CONCERNED ONLY FOR HIMSELF; ON A CLEAR DAY YOU COULD SEE HIS EGO FIVE MILES AWAY...

SO! HOW ARE YOU MATE?

PEA ALE

SLAP!

.AH! NOW WE'RE COMING TO THE KIND OF CONVERSATION I REALLY *ENJOY!*

...BUT, THERE'S A HAPPY ENDING. BECAUSE GARY MADE IT BACK. THERE WERE TEARS AND THERE WERE REGRETS...UNPAID BILLS (INCLUDING MINE)... -BUT THAT'S ANOTHER STORY!

IT WAS TOUGH -AT FIRST HE RESISTED.

HYPNOTIZE WITH ANY T.V. SET 1st EVENING OR MONEY BACK

LOOK DEEP INTO MY EYES... DEEP ...DEEP!

:GULP: IS...IS IT GONNA HURT?

IT TOOK TIME TO RE-ADJUST.

IS GARY PISSED, OR MERELY ALIENATED?

HE HAD A LOT OF INNER HOSTILITY TO UNRAVEL..

BACK ROW | BALCONY

OH GARY 'VE BEEN LONGING TO SEE THAT FILM. LET'S GO IN NOW.

THESE HYPNOTIC LIGHT RAYS WILL PUT YOU IN A RECEPTIVE FRAME OF MIND TO RECEIVE MY ANTI-HUMAN PROPAGANDA!

MR "NICE GUY" HAD TO RISK BEING OPEN AND DIRECT...

FOR A LONG WHILE NOW WE HAVE SEARCHED THE SOLAR SYSTEM FOR THE ONE WHO COULD HELP US! FINALLY WE SUCCEEDED! YOU ARE THE ONE!

YOU'RE INSANE MURDOCH! GET A GRIP ON YOURSELF BEFORE THEY THROW YOU OUT OF THE STAMP SOCIETY!

AND EVENTUALLY HE REALISED HE DIDN'T NEED TO PRETEND ANY MORE: -IT WAS OKAY TO JUST BE HIMSELF!

NO, EDWIN! WHEN YOU GO, YOU WILL LEAVE NOTHING BEHIND... I AM GOING WITH YOU!

I'D STILL ADORE YOU EVEN IF WE'D MET IN A FISH MARKET! -AND BY THE WAY, THE NAME'S GARY.

MEANWHILE, BACK IN THE PRESENT MOMENT..

THE UNKNOWN. -BARMY ISN'T IT ?

IT'S THE LATEST THING!

The End.

DR. CALIGARI WILL BE OPENING ANOTHER CASE HISTORY IN A FEW WEEKS TIME. THE THEME MUSIC TO THIS SERIES LOONY TUNES, IS NOW AVAILABLE IN MOST GOOD RECORD STORES

♪ ♫ ♪

DREAM HOME EXH...

Down in OLYMPIA, A SPOT OF POPULAR CAPITALISM IS TAKING PLACE...

Domestic Appliances
Leisure Bogs
D.I.Y. Art Pavilion
Gardening
100% Mortgage

ACTUALLY, WE'RE SCOUTING ROUND FOR SOME ART IN THE HOME.

ARE YOU FIRST-TIME BUYERS, REFURNISHING, REFURBISHING OR JUST LOOKING AROUND?

I UNDERSTAND THE CENTRE FEATURE OF THE VILLAGE IS THE ARTS COUNCIL'S *LIVING ART PAVILION*, PRESENTING A WIDE RANGE OF CONTEMPORARY WORK IN A VARIETY OF DOMESTIC SETTINGS.

THAT'S RIGHT! CRAZY PEOPLE! - CRAZY, CRAZY PRICES! ...OVER TO YOU, LUKE.

Thanks Bill... OK- welcome to the fascinating world of Private Patronage. You know, people often ask me, Can pictures do anything for me or my home? Certainly they can. Pictures bring life to a room and impress it with personality- kill the lights, Bill- Once in your home, a picture is part of your life. It can soothe, excite, amuse, tranquilise or simply decorate. It puts a 'window' on the wall both practically, metaphorically and spiritually.

SPIRIT GUIDE

For yesterday's youth with today's mortgage, a carefully chosen picture can brighten up a bed-sitter, or studio flat, as we artists like to call it...

...and, for the connoisseur, a well-placed canvas lends Elegance in the drawing-room

Can you please tell me the best way of removing the paint without damaging the canvas underneath?

How's about an 'important' picture in a traditional dining-room?

HAIR DRYER CHIC

PERSONALLY, I THINK ANGE SHOULD HAVE GIVEN DEN THE BUM'S RUSH.

Perhaps you'd like to Liven up a landing

Highlight a hall

or provide atmosphere for a teenager's den'

Parent-free Zone

But if, like the poet, your abode hath no endurance and your endurance no abode, i.e. you don't actually have a posh pad, I guess you're gonna need help with the readies, so without further ado I'll hand you over to our loan-shark-in-residence...

THANKS LUKE,.. O.K.. AS MATISSE SAID, I SEE BEFORE ME A WARDROBE...

DISCONTINUED

F. GRAY

INTRODUCING THE MEDIA BRATS
—THEY'RE REAL COOL CATS!

O.K. SHARON— I'M OUT TO LUNCH. BACK AT 4·30.

BAFTA 1986 love Dickie x

COMMISSIONING EDITOR Bright Ideas Dept.

THE CONCEPT CAN'T FAIL, JOHNNY — THE SHOW WILL HAVE EVERY **BUZZWORD** THAT WENT INTO THE '80s BLENDER!

CHOMP. CHOMP

SAY WAITER! —THERE'S A FLY IN MY 501's!

STARS...CHAT... HI -TECH... BAD TASTE...

...WE'RE TALKING **MEGA-RATINGS** HERE, JOHNNY...

HOW DO YOU ENVISAGE IT **WORKING**?

THINK OF IT! ANYONE FROM **BACH** TO **YUL BRYNNER**! **DOSTOEVSKY** TO **ARTHUR KOESTLER**!...

GOOD QUESTION!...WE'VE GOT THREE MEDIUMS, A TRANCE PIANIST, AN AUTOMATIC WRITER AND A TELEPATH WHO CAN TRANSFER **THOUGHT** ON ONTO **VIDEO**!

YEAH—WE COULD HAVE THEM RISING OUT OF A MIST OF **DRY ICE**!

ALL THE PANELISTS WILL HAVE TO DO IS IDENTIFY THE FAMOUS **STIFFS**..

WE THOUGHT WE'D CALL IT "THIS IS YOUR **AFTERLIFE**"..

RUSTLE

SORRY, BOYS — I DON'T THINK IT WOULD WORK... QUESTIONS OF COPYRIGHT, TABOO ETC.— NICE TRY THOUGH... CAN I HAVE THE BILL PLEASE, MARIO?

OH WELL, AT LEAST WE GOT A **SLAP-UP FEED** OUT OF IT!

YEAH—I THINK I'LL DO A **LIFESTYLE** PIECE FOR THE REVIEW SECTION INSTEAD.

OPEN

©1986 BIFF PRODUCTS

YAH—IT'LL BE A TRANSGRESSION OF EVERYTHING OBVIOUS, YET WEARABLE ENDLESSLY...

VIDEO DATING Join modern new style agency and find that special friend/partner through video. No more blind dates, just

BLIND DATA

not a toy!

Each boy gave her his heart
—— and a choice to make!

Knowledge and experience in computer-aided graphics and simulation would be an advantage

UNFORTUNATELY, NEVILLE (LEFT) THOUGHT HE WAS THE CAT'S NUTS..

HAW-HAW! THESE HOMBRES WON'T WORRY YOU AGAIN, MS. JULIE!

GOD! YOU'RE SO POSSESSIVE! THAT'S MY BACK-UP BAND, YOU CLOT!

BUT, BENEATH THE BRASH ROLE-PLAYING, HE WAS SEARCHING FOR APPROVAL.

O.K.—I ADMIT IT... I was a mug over birds and booze — BUT WE MUST CAST DIFFERENCES ASIDE FOR THE GOOD OF ALL PERSONKIND!

SO?—DO YOU WANT A TAXI OR A CONCORDAT?

KEN HAD CHARM, BUT ALSO AN ANNOYING TENDENCY TO TALK THROUGHOUT FILMS.

NON JE NE M'APPELLE PAS MONSIEUR RAMBO

—WONDER IF MY HEAD'S BLOCKING THE SUBTITLES?

SSHH!

—BASICALLY, HE GETS MANGLED IN THE SPIN-DRYER AFTER THE CAR-CHASE... OF COURSE, THESE EVENTS CANNOT BE ISOLATED AS SIGNIFIEDS FROM—

PLUS, HIS HYPER-ACTIVE LIFESTYLE SOON PALLED...

WELL—THAT WAS A TASTY SNACK. SHALL WE GO ALL-NIGHT CLUBBING?

HOLD ON—LET ME WALK OFF THE PAELLA FIRST.

...NEXT CAME DAVE... AT FIRST, IT WAS ALL HEARTS AND FLOWERS..

SOME DAY I'D LOVE TO PAINT YOU, JULIE —YOU HAVE AN EAGERNESS— AN AWARENESS OF LIFE I'D LIKE TO CAPTURE ON CANVAS!

YOU'D BETTER GO— I'VE A DEADLINE TO MEET!

PONG

© 1986 BIFF PRODUCTS

IN THE STREET OF **1000 IDEAS**, THAT'S WHERE YOU FIND **ALL THE YOUNG DUDES**

IMPACT ROGER..

OPEN

Patisserie

—SO OUT GO THE FUDDY-DUDDY DUFFLE COATS AND IN COMES DESIGNER-WEAR RELEVANCE...

Somewhere in the move, a huge mirror got broken. That, too, became crucial: to the shop's new interior.

CLICK

OH HI!—MIND IF I JOIN YOU FOR A LOW-FAT ECLAIR?

SURE!—I'M ALMOST FINISHED HERE... SO—HOW'S THINGS?

GENUINE SUEDETTE JACKET, CIRCA 1958

..AWESOME..

NEW YORK IS **OUT**..**RIO** IS WHERE IT'S HAPPENING...

NOT BAD, NOT BAD—I'M TRYING TO GET BACKERS FOR MY VIDEO NOVEL ABOUT FOUR STREET-WISE KIDS WHO ARE DANCE CRAZY.....YOURSELF?

OH—THIS'N'THAT...I'M REVAMPING THE LABOUR PARTY, PATENTING 2 NEW PHONE LINES, WRITING A PIECE ON CROSS-OVER DRESS AT ASCOT.....

..IT'LL BE A SIT-COM SET IN AN ESTATE AGENTS...

SQUELCH

.....AND CHOREOGRAPHING DAVE CLARK'S **ENNUI EXPRESS**, BASED ON THE RELATIONSHIP BETWEEN SARTRE AND SIMONE DE BEAUVOIR—VERY LEFT BANK.

SLURP

I HEAR THEY'RE AUDITIONING LULU AND SIR JOHN GIELGUD...

WELL—ID BETTER DASH—GOT TO SEE RICHARD BRANSON ABOUT THE REMOVAL OF SOME BULKY HOUSEHOLD REFUSE.

O.K.—CATCH YOU LATER YEAH?—AND **HANG LOOSE**, AS WE DON'T SAY ANY MORE!

DIDN'T THEY DECIDE TO TAKE ADVANTAGE OF AN OLD STEEL GIRDER SHELVING SYSTEM BY TURNING IT INTO A FEATURE?

OH-OH-DRY SCALP!.

Patisserie

..THE WAY THINGS LOOK IS THE WAY THINGS ARE... ...ER...

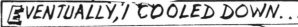

began by taking the basic share-a-flat sitcom structure and turning it inside out

ANYONE FANCY GOING OUT TO A *LATE NIGHT FILM?*

—DEPENDS WHICH ONE.

♪ÄR DET DE'HAER DU KALLAR KÄRLEK..

How to see ironing in a new light

HOW ABOUT STUDIO 3? —"A MARVELLOUSLY SPARE INCURSION INTO MODERN MANNERS, INFORMED WITH TRAGIC WIT.."

AH — A SPOT OF DISCREPANCY THERE · IT'S DESCRIBED HERE AS ANOTHER WILFULLY WEARISOME MESS OF CLICHES...

♪NÃO SEJAS MAU PARA MIM..

OKAY THEN — HOW ABOUT *'DREGS'* "...SET IN A RUN-DOWN FUTURISTIC LANDSCAPE, THE ACTION FOLLOWS THE FORTUNES OF FOUR YOUNG MISFITS... ...THE FINAL SHOOT-OUT IN THE DESERTED SUPERMARKET IS SURELY A METAPHOR FOR—

I WISH THEY WOULDN'T GIVE THE PLOT AWAY...NO POINT IN SEEING IT IF YOU KNOW THE *ENDING!*

♪..I BIN AWAY FOR FAR TOO LONG..♪

NOT AT ALL....IT'S WRONG TO ASSUME THAT A WORK HAS ONLY *ONE MEANING*... REVIEWS ARE MERELY GUIDES DEALING IN *SUPER- -FICIAL READINGS*, ALLOWING US ACCESS TO THE *DEEPER STRUCTURES* OF THE *TEXT*...

♪..MŸN LIEFDE IS AS EEN WIND-MOLEN..

OH GOOD— THIS IS THE EXCITING BIT!

..ONCE AGAIN THE SONGS HAVE ENCHANTED AN ENTIRE CONTINENT— NOW IT'S TIME TO HEAR FROM THE *NATIONAL PANELS*...

COME IN SWEDEN, —YOUR VOTES, PLEASE.

GOOD EEFNING, TERRY. WELL, AS EVER, IT'S A DIFFICULT CHOICE —THERE ARE AS MANY OPINIONS AS THERE ARE SONGS, ...IN A SENSE IT'S A *CRISIS OF CRITICISM*..WE MUST QUESTION THE NOTION OF *CONSENSUS*..

♪..DIE ZEIT IST EINSAM...

I SEE THE COMPUTERISED SCORING SYSTEM'S UP THE SPOUT AS PER USUAL

100% SHAG·PILE

© 1986 BIFF PRODUCTS

BOX 13 TO FAME

A TOP CONTESTANT EXPLAINS...

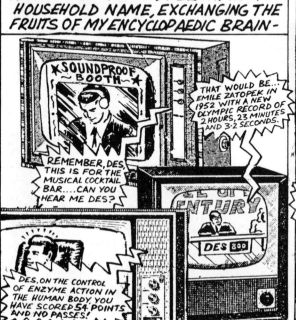

© 1985 BIFF PRODUCTS

© 1986 BIFF PRODUCTS.

SLAM!

BUT, AS ST. AUGUSTINE SAYS, WHAT IS TIME – OH, HE'S GONE...

WHOOSH!

NATURALLY, FRICTIONS DEVELOPED, BOTH AT WORK –

2LO CALLING...

Local Radio

WHERE HAVE YOU BEEN? I'VE HAD TO READ THE WEATHER FORECAST TEN TIMES ALREADY!

SORRY – THE CAR BROKE DOWN ON THE M.1.

VICKY! FORGIVE ME! I PROMISE I'LL CHANGE!

– AND OUTSIDE.

HMM – IS THIS A CRY FOR HELP OR FOR A KICK UP THE BUTT?

2ND GREAT YEAR! NO SEXISM PLEASE, WE'RE COMMUNITY WORKERS 8PM NIGHTLY "We laughed we cried"

AT FIRST, I TRIED HIM ON AUTO-SUGGESTION..

YOU ARE AN EXTREMELY PUNCTUAL PERSON YOU ARE AN EXTREMELY PUNCTUAL PERSON YOU ARE AN EXTREMELY PUNCTUAL PERSON YOU ARE AN EXTREMELY PUNCTUAL PERSON YOU ARE AN EXTREMELY PUNCTUAL PERSON YOU ARE AN

STUPENDOUS BARGAIN!

FOLLOWING IT UP WITH GUIDED FANTASIES...

WHAT'S HAPPENING NOW, PAUL – ARE YOU FOCUSSING?

THE BUS IS STUCK IN TRAFFIC ...NOW AT THE STATION...THERE'S A QUEUE.... EVERYONE WANTS TO BUY TICKETS WITH CREDIT CARDS..

AND FINALLY, MORE DYNAMIC TECHNIQUES...

RIGHT, PAUL, I'VE BOOKED YOU IN FOR A SYMPOSIUM AT 9.30, A CHAT SHOW AT 11, A WORKING LUNCH ACROSS TOWN AT 12.40, THEN 6 CONFERENCES IN 3 HOURS AT DIFFERENT VENUES! OKAY? – PAUL – WHERE ARE YOU?

AND NOW HE'S ON THE HOME STRETCH.

YOU'RE THREE MINUTES LATE, DOC', – I DEMAND A PERCENTAGE REFUND!

GOD! THERE'S NOTHING WORSE THAN THE PIETY OF A REFORMED CHARACTER!

I SHOULDN'T HAVE STAYED UP WATCHING ALL THOSE WORLD CUP SPECIALS!

BAH! I'VE GOT ABOUT AS MUCH SENSE OF DIRECTION AS A MOTH IN A LAMPSHADE!

HE HAS INNER DIALOGUE THE ANCIENTS CALLED IT

WRITER'S BLOCK

Entertaining, and sometimes only too familiar,* account of blank days at the typewriter.

* You're not kidding. —Ed.

THAT FRIDGE IS DRIVING ME SLOWLY NUTS!

DRONE

BLANK

THIS IS THE ABRASIVE EIGHTIES — NO-ONE GOES FOR FIRST-PERSON INTROSPECTION ANY MORE...

I SHOULD'VE GONE TO GLASTONBURY WITH THE OTHERS!

SILENT

TRISTAN TOOK A MENTAL LAXATIVE IN THE FORM OF A STROLL ROUND N.W.I. — BUT...

BUS STOP

famous writer ROBERT LOUIS STEVENSON 1831-84 lived here

MICHAEL CAINE STOOD HERE IN ALFIE 1965

AT THIS RATE, THE ONLY PLAQUE I'LL EVER HAVE IS IN MY MOUTH!

He began to pace up and down, head bowed and then forcibly drew up short, facing at last the crux of the problem, the very heart of the matter.

I'M BETWEEN PROJECTS, THAT'S ALL... CREATIVE HIATUS IT'S CALLED.

HUH! LOOKS MORE LIKE HERNIA HIATUS TO ME!

SA! PRICES SLASH

38's

Back home, and a call from Harry. He's not one of those agent-tycoons whose every other word to you is interrupted by an international telephone call, a telex requiring an immediate reply, or a motor-cycle courier bringing last-minute contracts or whatever.

TRISTAN?.. LISTEN... I'VE GOT A PROVISIONAL ACCEPTANCE ON A SERIES! ....HELLO?... YOU STILL THERE?....CAN YOU COME UP A COUPLE OF DUMMY DRAFTS BY FRIDAY?

JJ

HARRY—I KEEP TELLING YOU, —I WANT HEADLINES, NOT DEADLINES!!..I'LL SEE WHAT I CAN DO.....

....HOW DO THEY WANT IT?—ELEGANTLY PASSIONATE OR TAUTLY CRAFTED?

POUND-POUND-CLATTER-DING....

—THINK I'LL JUST PUT THE KETTLE ON...

...THAT'S RIGHT JIMMY-THE LAD LIKES TO RUN AT THE DEFENCES.

IT'S JUST A QUESTION OF MOTIVATION, THAT'S ALL.

THE CONSUMING INTERESTS OF
VIDEO VERA

TV of the future, NOW! +Free magazine rack stand!

WITH ONE OF THESE, I COULD GO TO THE JOBS FESTIVAL *AND* SEE THE WIMBLEDON FINAL.... ...DANCE AT LES'S PARTY AND STILL CATCH THE LIVE AID WEMBLEY GIG!

OOH WHAT A FINE DESTRUCTIVE LOB THAT WAS!

CAN I HELP YOU MADAM?

15% OF £349 =...

SALE

ER — JUST LOOKING, THANKS.

"A WHOLE NEW AREA OF CULTURAL AWARENESS MIGHT OPEN UP..."

I'LL TAKE 2 WENDERS AND A RESTORATION COMEDY; —DON'T BOTHER TO WRAP THEM.

GRUNT.

VIDEO CLUB MEMBERSHIP £...

HOW MUCH IS THIS ONE?

FUCK KNOWS MARK..

CAN THAT PIECE OF MISJUDGEMENT HAVE COST THE AMERICAN THE MATCH, DAN?

A WISE CHOICE — STRICTLY VIDEO FOR THE AUDIOPHILE, THAT ONE-TOUCH CONTROLS. (THINKS: I BLOODY HATE THIS JOB)

"-BUT, WOULD IT TAKE OVER MY LIFE?"

DID I REMEMBER TO SET IT FOR 'READY STEADY GO'?

ICE

DON'T WORRY — YOU NEVER ACTUALLY WATCH IT — YOU JUST RECORD IT ONE WEEK AND WIPE IT THE NEXT.

"-AND IT MIGHT CAUSE ARGUMENTS IN THE HOUSE..."

FOR GOD'S SAKE, DAVE, YOU CAN'T SERIOUSLY WANT TO RECORD THE INDOOR BOWLS?

TYPICAL ARIES!

—AND WITH THIS ONE YOU ALSO GET 14-DAY, 5-PROGRAMME TIMER, FREEZE FRAME AND MEMORY SEARCH FACILITIES AS STANDARD...

LISTEN — YOU CAN WATCH 'ELEVENTH HOUR' ANY WEEK!

"BESIDES, I'M USELESS WITH MACHINES.."

OH NO! I SET IT FOR 4 AM INSTEAD OF 4 PM!

HISS!

—SO, WHAT'S IT TO BE THEN? — EASY CREDIT OR THE READIES?

SORRY — I'M GONNA HAVE TO THINK ABOUT IT.

QUIET PLEASE LADIES AND GENTLEMEN... —AND YOU, DAN HO-HO-HO!

THAT'S OKAY... BUT REMEMBER.. PROCRASTINATION IS THE THIEF OF TIME.. —PUSH OFF.

© 1986 BIFF PRODUCTS.

The politics of sound.

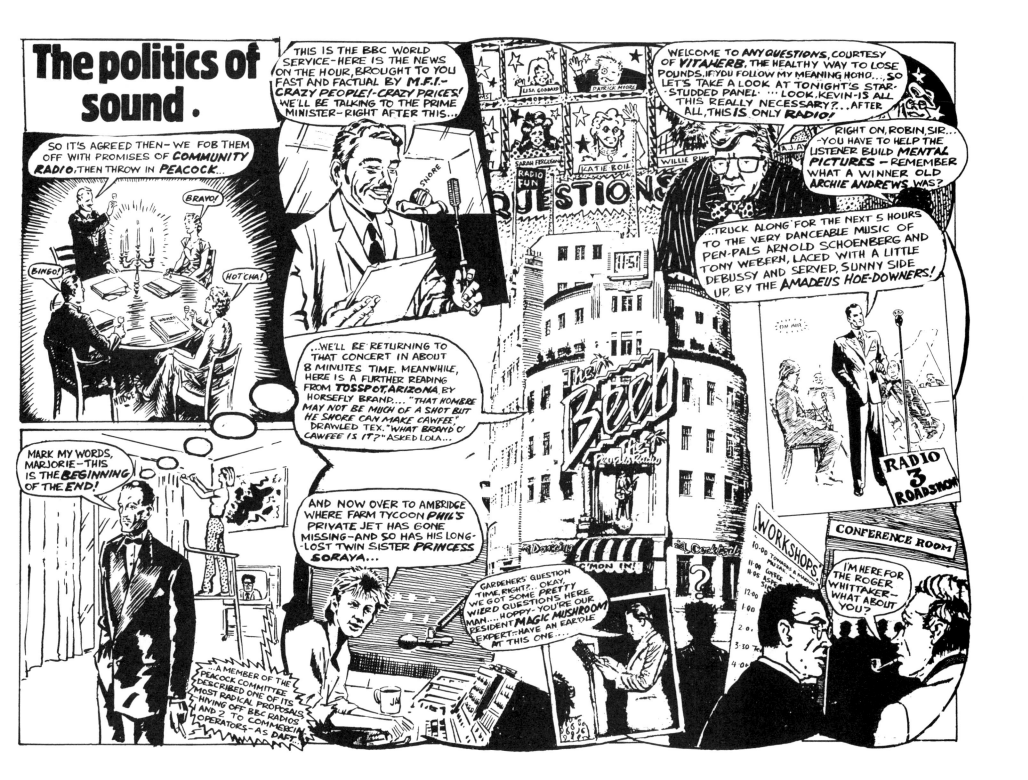

Media File.....

THE HOST WAS A SOCIAL PSYCHOLOGIST, THE GUESTS WERE A BUNCH OF STRANGERS... TOGETHER THEY WERE EMBARKING ON:

ADVENTURES IN CONVERSATION

I'M KIM TORONTO: I'M A CREATIVE ACCOUNTANT.

STEVE 'N' ANGIE'S SOIRÉES TEND TO BE WILD YET SOPHISTICATED AFFAIRS.... —HOPE I SPARKLE!

HURRY UP —I'M STARVING!

"INSIDE, THINGS WERE BUBBLING UNDER..."

YAH— THE SAFETY CELL IS SURROUNDED BY IMPACT-ABSORBING CRUMPLE ZONES, AFFORDING FORMIDABLE PROTECTION...

HA-HA!

BRILLIANT!

DING-DONG!

"...WITH A SPOT OF BODY LANGUAGE AND STATUS EXCHANGE..."

TRY A DROP O' THIS, ME DUCK — IT'S FROM THE FIRST VINEYARD ACROSS THE ALPS — ONE FOOT IN THE EARTH, THE OTHER ONE IN THE SKY, THEY SAY.

I HATE PEOPLE IN MIRRORED SHADES!

"—BUT THESE SEEMED AN AMIABLE ENOUGH CREW..."

WELCOME ABOARD! WE'RE JUST ENGAGING IN SOME LIGHT PLEASANTRIES BEFORE GETTING STUCK INTO A HEATED DEBATE!

IS THAT THE DISHWASHER OR AN ERIC DELANEY DRUM SOLO?

RUMBLE!

WHICH CAMERA ARE WE ON?

.....AND YOU GET A PERSONALISED LEATHER WALLET WITH A BUILT-IN CALCULATOR....

"..AND IT WASN'T LONG BEFORE STEVE ARRIVED WITH THE **CHOW**."

TAKE A PEW, EVERYONE. FOR STARTERS THERE'S A FORM OF **BRIOCHE** THAT HAS CONQUERED THE WHOLE OF ITALY, FOLLOWED BY QUICHE AND 3 VEG. THE POTATOES ARE MORE-ISH, THE SALADS LESS SO, BUT HOPEFULLY, FORGIVENESS WILL BE IN ORDER AFTER THE EXQUISITE KNICKERBOCKER GLORIES!

SNAP

WOW!

MMM!

OUTA SIGHT!

"LATER, THE WINE FLOWED, AND WITH IT, THE EXCHANGE OF IDEAS..."

-I FOUND IT A THIN COMEDY, I'M AFRAID.

REALLY? —BUT, HOW COULD YOU NOT WEEP WITH AGAMEMNON?

MY MOUSTACHE IS ALL THAT KEEPS ME FROM FALLING APART.

"...AND I BEGAN TO FEEL AT HOME, CONTENT TO BE A PICKER-UP OF CRUMBS AT LEARNING'S TABLE."

FOR ME, NOTHING QUITE EQUALS THE FRIENDLY WARMTH OF A D.I.Y. KITCHEN UNIT...

..MIND YOU, FOR WEEKS THE WATER SYSTEM HASN'T BEEN RIGHT AND NOW THE BOILER HAS STOPPED WORKING...

?

FOAM

Geigfrie Lager Kit

I LIKE HOME-BREW, BUT IT DOESN'T LIKE ME.

Domesto Retsina

"OH—I SUPPOSE I MADE THE ODD **FAUX-PAS**..."

BASICALLY I FIND ALL COUNTRY & WESTERN MUSIC REACTIONARY CRAP.

IS THAT SO? WELL, WE HAPPEN TO HAVE THE ENTIRE DOLLY PARTON COLLECTION AND I'M THE SECRETARY OF THE LOCAL LABOUR PARTY!

...BUT, ON THE WHOLE, I THOUGHT I COPED VERY WELL. —HOW WAS YOUR EVENING?

SSHH, NORMAN... —I'M HAVING AN IMPORTANT DREAM.

SOME DAYS THE LIGHTS ARE ALWAYS ON **RED** WHEN YOU'RE **WORKING FROM HOME** STARRING KEN VANCE, FREE? -LANCE.

FUNNY- I SPEND A THIRD OF MY LIFE ASLEEP YET I NEVER REMEMBER MY DREAMS... I WONDER WHAT TIME IT IS...

I DIDN'T SPEAK.

IT'S 9 O'CLOCK HERE IN LONDON ON THIS GREY OVERCAST MORN...

I'LL JUST GLANCE AT THE PAPER, THEN MAKE A **START**!

TWANG!

I HOUR LATER

-ONE LAST CUPPA, THEN I'LL DEF-**GRRR**!! YOU'D THINK IN THIS HI-TECH ERA THEY COULD COME UP WITH A NON-EXPLODING CARTON!

CLEAN SHIRT

SPLAT! WUPP!

10 MINUTES INTO THE FUTURE... BRRR-BRR...

KEN... HI! ARE YOU FREE FOR THE SUB-COMMITTEE ON TUESDAY?

SOMETIMES I THINK WE'RE THE MEETINGS GENERATION!

SURE, SUE, -THAT'LL BE FINE (SIGH).

5 MINUTES LATER

".. THERE ARE ECHOES HERE OF KLUGE, RIVETTE - EVEN THE YOUTHFUL ROHMER, BUT ONLY ECHOES.."

CLATTER-CLATTER!

I'M NOT IN THE MOOD; MAYBE A WALK WILL CLEAR MY BRAIN.

LET'S FACE IT- YOU COULD CALL ME LAZY WITHOUT FEAR OF A SLANDER SUIT.

TRASH

THE SAME MORNING...

"-AUTEURISM NO LONGER PROVIDES AN ADEQUATE.."

GOLDARN IT!! -THE RIBBON'S ON THE BLINK- THERE'S PLANNED OBSOLESCENCE FOR YOU!

CLATTER-CLATTER- PLUNK!

KNOCK-KNOCK! (DOOR)

OH NO!

FOR NORMAN AND BLANCHE —

Patio living ends here!

DO YOU THINK THAT IF WE CALL IT A **BARBECUE** IT'LL BUCKET DOWN?

WELL, WE COULD ALWAYS RE-NAME IT AN **INDOOR PICNIC!**

AS ALWAYS, *THERE WERE* LAST-MINUTE PANICS

CAN YOU GET THAT, BLANCHE? — I'M AT A CRUCIAL STAGE WITH THIS TRIFLE!

DING-DONG!!

NO — YOU GO... I'VE STILL GOT 1½ HOURS OF PARTY TAPE TO FINISH.

HI! AM I THE FIRST TO ARRIVE?

BUT ONCE THINGS GOT GOING...

BIG DEAL!

WE GOT THIS BIRD AT THE ORGANIC BUTCHERS.

EXCUSE ME, DO YOU KNOW WHOSE DO THIS IS?

FOR ME, AN AESTHETIC CANNOT BE CONSTRUCTED IN A **VOID**...

I AGREE — WHICH COMMISSIONING EDITOR ARE YOU DEALING WITH BY THE WAY?

...PEOPLE LOOSENED UP —

ACTUALLY, I DON'T ENJOY PARTIES MUCH NOWADAYS.

SO... HOW'S THINGS ON YOUR PRODUCT PATCH?

YOU MUST BE STARTING YOUR MID-LIFE CRISIS.

SIZZLE

HOT DOGS

— NATTERING AWAY OVER A JAR OR TWO.

I UNDERSTAND MARION IS BRINGING ALONG A SELECTION OF HER COUNTRY WINES.

I DIDN'T REALISE SHE WAS INTO **NEIL YOUNG.**

SEEBACKROSCOPE

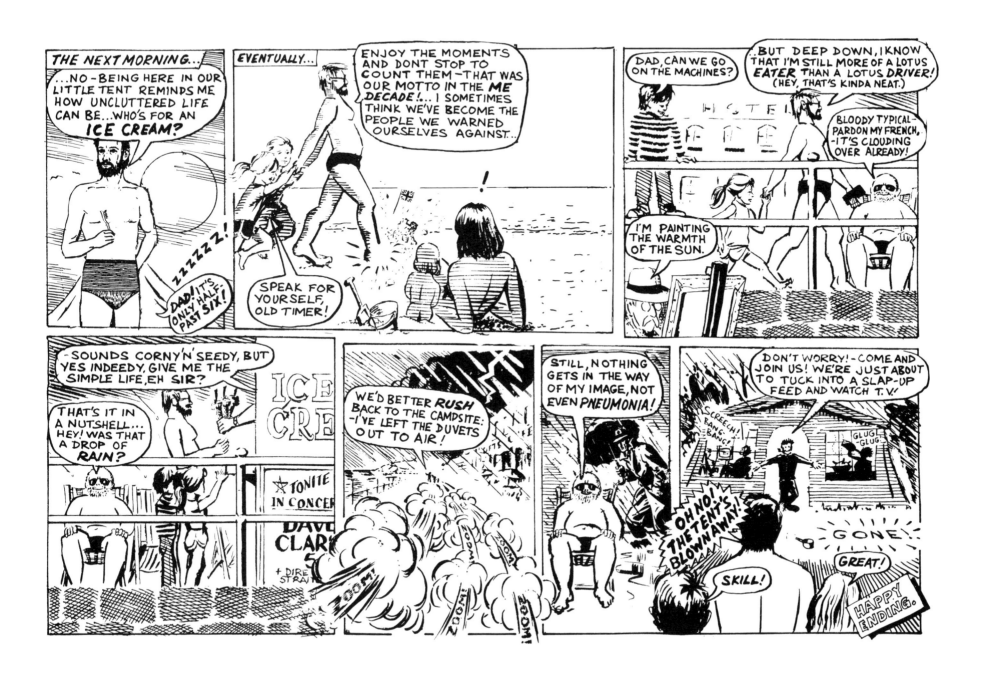

I APPLIED TO MY BOSS FOR TIME OFF IN POLPERRO.....

IT'S NOT FOR MASTERMIND, IS IT?

NO-I JUST WANT TO CATCH UP ON SOME GENERAL READING... I NEVER GOT PAST PAGE 40 OF '6 EXISTENTIALIST THINKERS'.

AT FIRST, THINGS WENT WELL...

HMM-ARCHITECTURE AS FROZEN MUSIC... AN INTERESTING CONCEPT.

OF COURSE, FREUD WAS UNDENIABLY PHALLOCENTRIC.

GREAT! AT LAST I'VE READ THE ALEXANDRIA QUARTET!

GOOD HEAVENS - THE DAILY OUTPUT OF FLATULENCE OF A SINGLE SHEEP COULD POWER A SMALL CAR FOR TWENTY MILES!

BUT, I OVER-DID IT AND HAD TO CALL THE DOCTOR..

I'M STARTING TO ANALYSE MY DREAMS WHILE I'M STILL ASLEEP, DOC... IT'S MY RIGHT HEMISPHERE I THINK.

YOU HAVE A MILD ATTACK OF INFORMATION OVERLOAD, THAT'S ALL...

YOU SHOULD TAKE THINGS MORE SLOWLY - GET PLENTY OF EXERCISE.

SO I DUG OUT THE OLD HEAP AND BEETLED OFF TO VISIT PALS.

SHEER DROP↓

IT GOT A BIT SOLITARY - I GUESS I NEED PEOPLE TO BOUNCE OFF!

I USED TO GET THE SAME WITH THE O.U. WHY NOT TRY SOME EVENING CLASSES?

REG HARRI

TRADITIONAL CELTIC PATTERN

SOME WEEKS LATER, BACK IN TOWN...

YES, I'M DOING DRAMA ON MONDAYS, POPULAR CULTURE ON WEDNESDAYS, AND ON FRIDAYS IT'S ASTRONOMY, -OR WAS IT ASTROLOGY?

WHAT IS THIS, SOME KIND OF SERIAL?

LIVE MUSIC FRIDAYS. Venoms Skiffle Group

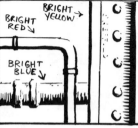

SEE YOU IN ALGEBRA TOMORROW, GAIL!

THAT SOUNDS DELIGHTFUL— I'LL TELL MILT WE'RE GOING

I REMEMBER YOU ♪

In Autumn, as the nights draw in and the weather turns colder, shopping from home makes more sense than ever, *Sorry, wrong story..*

TAKE TWO : THIS YOUNGISH COUPLE ARE ON THEIR WAY TO THE BOTTLE-BANK WHEN THEY BUMP INTO THE POSTMAN..

LOOKS LIKE THE USUAL PILE OF BROWN ENVELOPES.

GUESS WHAT—WE'VE BEEN INVITED TO OUR COLLEGE REUNION!

WILL THEY BE MAKING A T.V. DOCUMENTARY ABOUT IT?

IT'LL BE REALLY INTERESTING TO SEE WHAT'S BECOME OF EVERYONE — WE WERE A PRETTY *WILD BUNCH!*

COMING TO THE PYJAMA DANCE TONIGHT, V'RON?

NO CHANCE,— I'VE GOT TO SCRIPT THE THIRD ACT OF MY *GRITTY REALIST DRAMA!*

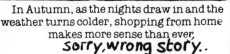

3 WEEKS LATER— THE BIG DAY!

WE'RE TRAVELLING THROUGH *TIME* AS WELL AS *SPACE!*

IT'S STRAIGHT AHEAD SIR... HEY, AREN'T YOU THE FUNNY LITTLE BLOKE WHO USED TO RUN THE *FOLK CLUB?*

ROLL UP! GET YOUR REUNION T-SHIRTS AND SOUVENIR PROGRAMMES!

BRRM... BRRM...

SON...

IMAGE...

SON ET IMAGE...

RIEN...

THERE HE GOES AGAIN THE OLD WANKER.... NUBILE FEMALES APPENDED TO PSEUDO-RADICAL WORD-GAMES!

LA FEMME - LA USINE OU LE PAYSAGE?

IT'S WORSE THAN THE SEXIST AD IMAGES HE PURPORTS TO CONDEMN!

YOU'RE COLONISING THE TEXT WITH YOUR OWN PURITANICAL HANG-UPS - FASCIST!

WOW - ZAT IZ NICE, BÉBÉ...

THERE IS NO SUCH THING AS AN INNOCENT IMAGE.

YOU SHOULD NOT ALLOW YOUR OEDIPAL GUILT TO IMPEDE THE DISTANCING OF PLEASURE FROM A POLITICAL RE-READING OF THAT PLEASURE.

FIN

WELL, FAR FROM BEING SOPORIFIC, I FOUND GODARD, AS EVER, A CHALLENGING SPRINGBOARD FOR DISCUSSION...

Mr. McCabe's Jumpers courtesy of MARKS & SPARKS

Z Z Z Z Z

BRRR-BRRR!

THE TRUE AND MOVING STORY OF ONE MAN'S FIGHT TO REACH A *DEADLINE!*

KEN—I HAVEN'T RECEIVED YOUR PAPER YET—I WAS HOPING TO GET IT TYPE-SET AND COLLATED FOR TONIGHT'S CONFERENCE!

GREAT SCOTT! —I COULD HAVE SWORN IT WAS NEXT MONTH!

WELL..I..ER..SENT IT LAST WEEK!....I'LL HAVE TO BRING A ROUGH DRAFT!

FINE! WHICH TRAIN WILL YOU CATCH?

ZERO MINUS 10 HOURS.

POUND-POUND-CLATTER-CLATTER

8 HOURS...

JUST PUT IT DOWN THERE. —THANKS.

POUND-CLATTER-

7 HOURS...

CLATTER...

BRRR-BRRR!

IF IT'S FOR ME, I'M NOT IN!

LOOK...CAN YOU GIVE MY APOLOGIES TO THE MEETING? SOMETHING'S COME UP...

SAY, KEN, YOUR TRAIN LEAVES IN 20 MINUTES!

TYPE-TYPE.

AT THE STATION—3 HOURS TO GO.

I KNEW IT!!

LONG QUEUE

...AND CAN YOU TELL ME THE TIME OF THE LAST TRAIN TO SAN FERNANDO

TICKETS

EXCUSE ME — IS THAT SEAT TAKEN?

GOOD MORNING, THIS IS THE CHIEF STEWARD. THE BAR AND BUFFET WILL BE OPEN SHORTLY FOR THE SALE OF TEA, COFFEE, DRINKS, HOT AND COLD SNACKS...

PARDON?

YES — I RECKON IT'S THE *LEFT* BEHIND THESE TRAVELLING CRIMINAL ELEMENTS...

INCLUDING TOASTED EGG, TOASTED BACON, TOASTED CHEESE SANDWICHES

SHUFFLE

RIOT

OH NO — A TALKATIVE TYPE... AND *I'VE* GOT MY BACK TO THE ENGINE!

MAYBE I SHOULD GO INTO A *FIRST CLASS* CARRIAGE. I DISAGREE ENTIRELY WITH SUCH OUTMODED ELITISM BUT THIS IS AN *EMERGENCY!* — BESIDES, I MIGHT GET AWAY WITH IT!

..I MEAN, THEY'D BE MUGS NOT TO EXPLOIT THIS AS A MEANS OF *DESTABILISATION*..

OH YER — WE LOVED IT... ONLY WISH WE COULD HAVE STAYED LONGER...

EXCUSE ME — I HAVE THE SUDDEN URGE FOR AN ALL-DAY BREAKFAST!

SOPHIE — DON'T EAT CRISPS OFF THE FLOOR, DEAR.

I HOUR...

VE VISH TO SEE YOUR PAPERS...

PLEASE HAVE YOUR TICKETS READY FOR INSPECTION, — AND NO HIDING IN THE LAV...

1ST CLASS ONLY

BLAST! I WAS JUST GETTING INTO A RHYTHM!

R-RIP!

Imperial Typewriter

15 MINUTES...

I KNOW I WORK BETTER UNDER PRESSURE BUT THIS IS *CRAZY!*

Conference Paper Society on

WHERE TO, MATE?

CLATTER CLATTER...

...PROCRASTINATION, THEN, IN PSYCHO-ANALYTIC TERMS, CAN BE SEEN AS A DESIRE TO POSTPONE THE **MOMENT OF ARRIVING** IN ORDER TO SAVOUR FURTHER THE **PERMUTATIONS OF POSSIBILITY**. IRONICALLY, THE PLEASURE SO DERIVED IS A **MASOCHISTIC** ONE, THE PROCRASTINATOR FEELING ONLY **CONTEMPT** FOR HIMSELF AS THE SUBJECT OF THAT DESIRE...

WELL, KEN, I FOUND YOUR PAPER THE HIGHLIGHT OF THE CONFERENCE... MUST HAVE NEEDED A LOT OF *PREPARATION*.

— THE BAR AND BUFFET WILL BE CLOSING IN FIVE MINUTES SO GET A MOVE ON!

WELL — IT'S NO USE LEAVING THESE THINGS TILL THE *LAST MINUTE* IS IT? — HAVE A PEANUT.

You often see pictures of people riding in taxis along famous streets.

LUNCHTIME...

VICTOR'S OFF SICK (SO HE SAYS), —CAN YOU COVER THE SCHOOL PRIZE-DAY?

GOD, I FEEL LIKE A CHAMELEON!

WELL, I'M DOWN TO DO A MUSIC ITEM, A RETIREMENT AND A MIDWEEK REPLAY, —BUT I'LL TRY...

IN THIS CHANGING WORLD OF OURS, THERE ARE SOME QUALITIES THAT SHOULD NEVER CHANGE....

MUST GET ON TO COUNTY HALL ABOUT THIS CEILING...

...I'M TALKING ABOUT HARD WORK. LOYALTY. DEDICATION. ENDEAVOUR. AND PERHAPS NO-ONE EMBODIES THESE QUALITIES MORE—

—THAN YOURS TRULY. AS AN OLD BOY OF THIS SCHOOL AND NOW A SUCCESSFUL INTERNATIONAL ARMS DEALER...

The taxi keeps quite still. It is really the picture on the screen that is moving.

I'M NO MERE CAB DRIVER— I'M A POET OF THE NIGHT!

"THUD" "THUD" "TWANG" "WHOOP"

NO, WE HAVEN'T GOT A CONTRACT YET—WE'RE MORE INTERESTED IN GETTING THE SOUND RIGHT—NOT JUMPING ON ANY BANDWAGON.

WE DO A LOT OF BENEFITS LOCALLY. THE MUSIC IS JUST PART OF OUR WIDER CONCERNS.

WOULD YOU LIKE SOME TEA WHILE YOU HEAR THE DEMOS?

RIGHT...

WOULD YOU SAY THAT, AS AN ALL-WOMAN BAND, YOUR OPPOSITIONAL STANCE MAY BE COMPROMISED BY POSITIVE DISCRIMINATION?

MEANWHILE...

insert pic here.

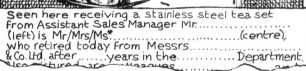

Seen here receiving a stainless steel tea set from Assistant Sales Manager Mr................. (left) is Mr/Mrs/Ms*.........................(centre), who retired today from Messrs.................... & Co. ltd. after........years in the.............Department. Also pictured are.....colleagues.................

AT THE QUIET END OF THE DAY...

SAME AGAIN JANICE? I EXPECT YOU'RE GLAD TO BE FINISHED.

FINISHED? I'VE STILL GOT A SOCCER DERBY AND MY EATING OUT COLUMN TO DO!

I THINK I'LL APPLY FOR THAT JOB IN LOCAL RADIO.

SO...YOU'RE A JOURNALIST, EH? I COULD TELL YOU A FEW STORIES AND NO MISTAKE. THERE WAS THIS REP I MET IN READING....

TAP -TAP -TAP..

Of course, my happiness couldn't last: our relationship hit a rocky patch.

WHAT DID YOU SAY?

GO FIND YOURSELF ANOTHER EARTH-MOTHER...I'M SICK OF MASSAGING YOUR EGO!

SQUEAL OF BRAKES ETC.

It was then that I found out who my real friends were.

OH, HI— C'MON IN MAN... DO YOU NEED TO CRASH ON OUR FLOOR AWHILE?

YOU'RE JUST IN TIME FOR THREE HOURS OF ME LOONIN' ABOUT ON THE GUITAR!

But I'm a survivor, and I was soon back in the thick of things..

...NO, THURSDAY'S OUT— I'M RENOVATING LARRY'S HOUSE. FRIDAYS I WORK BEHIND THE BAR AT THE DOG AND BISHOP...SATURDAY, THAT'S AN ALL-DAY PARTY THROWN BY AN ÉMIGRÉE COUNTESS...HOW ABOUT SUNDAY?—NO, HANG ON —I'M SEEING MY GURU IN BRIGHTON...

MAYBE I'LL STAY IN AND WASH MY HAIR.

...I CAN MEET YOU AFTER CHRISTMAS...

100% INDIAN COTTON

..before getting gripped by the WANDERLUST.

...THEN I GOT A LIFT FROM STAINES TO BELGRADE— FANTASTIC! WHEN DO WE REACH NEPAL? I HEAR THE CAFÉ LIFE IS EXCELLENT!

WE'D GET THERE A DAMN SIGHT SOONER IF THIS CRATE HAD A PROPER STEERING WHEEL!

28,000 WORDS LATER...

FINISHED AT LAST— ONE LONG PROTEST AGAINST MORTALITY! MAYBE THIS WILL EARN ME A WRITER-IN-RESIDENCE STINT SOMEWHERE.

IT'S ANOTHER SLEEPING BAG NOVEL— HARDLY BOOKER PRIZE MATERIAL... WHAT SHOULD I SAY?

TELL HIM THAT HIS WORK SHOWS MERIT BUT SUGGEST HE TRIES HISTORICAL ROMANCE OR CRIME THRILLERS!

—TALK TO YOU LATER...

LOVE BANDITS OF TIME. An explosive 2nd Novel.

AND FOR THE CHILDREN AND ALL WHO ARE *YOUNG AT HEART*, THERE'S A CLOWN ON THE PATIO!

ER-HEM... ACTUALLY I PREFER TO BE DESCRIBED AS A PERSON WITH *CIRCUS SKILLS*.

HEY DAD, TEDDY SAYS HE WANTS ANOTHER TEQUILA SUNRISE.

-SO FEEL FREE TO WANDER... BUT DON'T FORGET THE *SLIDE SHOW* AT 9.30!

VERILY, THESE TWO ARE THE ARMAND AND MICHAELA DENIS OF THE DOMESTIC ARTS...

9·30. THIS IS STEVE WALKING DOWN THE BEACH AFTER TREADING ON A SEA URCHIN.

WHAT FILMSTOCK WERE YOU USING, ANGIE?

THIS IS ON F.22 I PRESUME...

PSST! TIME TO MAKE AN EXCUSE AND LEAVE.

AND THIS IS- OH SORRY.. -LIGHTS PLEASE SOMEONE.

MEANWHILE.

WHY DON'T WE STROLL BACK TO THE FIRE AND CATCH THE DYING EMBERS?

GULP

LET ME EXPLAIN....IF A SPACESHIP IS APPROACHING THE *SPEED OF LIGHT*, IT WOULD ATTAIN *INFINITE MASS*, BUT TO AN OBSERVER BACK ON EARTH...NO-HANG ON...LET'S SEE... OF COURSE IT MAY BE ENTERING A *BLACK HOLE*, IN WHICH CASE..

YES-IT CERTAINLY MAKES ONE THINK.. ALL THOSE LONG AGO SIGNALS...IMAGES OF *ELSEWHERE*!

I WONDER IF THAT'S HALLEY'S COMET.

ONLY 168 SHOPPING DAYS TO SPRING.

TSK-THERE'S ALWAYS SOMEONE WHO SPOILS IT FOR EVERYONE ELSE.

CHANGE IS THE MOVING IMAGE OF *ETERNITY*, AS I ONCE WROTE,. OR WAS IT PLATO?

STEAM

HISSS...

SOUNDS MORE LIKE *PETRARCH* TO ME.. HE WAS A WALKING *FILING CABINET* YOU KNOW...

HERE ARE SOME DETAILS OF OUR MORE COMPACT ACCOMODATION, IDEAL FOR FIRST-TIME BUYERS, SECOND HOME USE OR AS INVESTMENT.

WE WILL OF COURSE BE PLEASED TO ACCOMPANY YOU ON AN INSPECTION OF ANY OF THESE..

FLASH SUIT →

THIS ISN'T DECEPTIVELY SPACIOUS, —IT'S A DOG-BOX!

WE BEG YOUR PARDON...WE NEVER PROMISED YOU A ROSE GARDEN.

CASH

SKILLFULLY CONVERTED? —THE ARCHITECT SHOULD BE DONE UNDER THE TRADES DESCRIPTIONS ACT!

AH —YOU'LL PROBABLY NOT GO A BUNDLE ON OUR MOCK-CLASSICAL RUIN THEN..

OH SORRY— THE AGENTS SAID IT WAS OKAY TO LOOK AROUND.

I KEEP TELLING THEM TO LET ME KNOW FIRST!

AT WORK..

HOW'S THE HOUSE-HUNTING GOING, JANE?

TERRIBLE!

HOWEVER YOU THINK YOUR HOME COULD BE IMPROVED, —KITCHEN, ATTIC, DOUBLE-GLAZING, CENTRAL HEATING ADDING A ROOM OR GARAGE, NOTHING BEATS THE BARGAINING POWER OF CASH..

I WOULDN'T BOTHER... ALL PROPERTY IS THEFT ANYWAY.

AND SO...

MAYBE WE NEED TO THINK ABOUT IT A BIT MORE... NO POINT IN RUSHING THINGS.

ANYWAY—IT'S NOT SO BAD HERE... OH NO!—WHO'S BEEN USING MY MUM'S NON-STICK PANS?

I'LL DO THE WASHING-UP TOMORROW IF I DON'T GET TOO TANKED UP TONIGHT.

WOKE UP THIS MORNIN'...

STARRING MR & MRS HAIRDRESSING SALON

WELL, AT THIS POINT WE WERE HOPING TO HAVE A TOP HORSE-BREEDER OR A QUIZ SHOW HOST WITH A BOOK TO PLUG...

CRUNCH

CRUNCH MUNCH

UNFORTUNATELY NONE OF THEM NEEDED THE MONEY BADLY ENOUGH TO GET UP AT THIS GODFORSAKEN HOUR...BUT IT'S VERY GOOD OF *SAMUEL BECKETT* TO STEP IN AT SUCH SHORT NOTICE..SAM-WELCOME TO BREAKFAST T.V!

SAM-YOU'VE BEEN WHINGEING ON ABOUT DEATH AND DESPAIR FOR OVER 40 YEARS NOW...DON'T YOU SOMETIMES FEEL YOU'RE MISSING OUT ON LIFE?

DO YOU WANT YOUR COFFEE IN THE BATH?

YES PLEASE.

I MEAN - YOUR CHARACTERS ARE ALL IN TERMINAL STATES.. DEATHBEDS, DUSTBINS - ALL WASHED UP. HAS THERE BEEN A LOT OF BEREAVEMENT IN YOUR LIFE?

NOT REALLY - I JUST LISTEN TO RADIO FOUR A LOT, THAT'S ALL..

SO WHY DON'T YOU WRITE SOME JOLLY STORIES - EVEN SOME ZANY STUFF?

FUNNY YOU SHOULD SAY THAT...CURRENTLY I'M WORKING ON A SIT-COM ABOUT THREE FLAT-SHARING WASHROOM ATTENDANTS AND THEIR CRAZY LANDLADY PLAYED BY IRENE HANDL.

WILLIAM WOOLLARD LOOK

THERE YOU GO.. ..I'M GONNA START MY HOOVERING NOW.

THANKS, HONEY.

YOU ONCE LIKENED YOUR OWN COUNTENANCE TO THAT OF A 3-MONTH-OLD POTATO DISCOVERED UNDER THE FRIDGE...HOW'S IT FEEL?

ACME

I THINK IT'S ESSENTIAL FOR THE ARTIST TO SUFFER - OR TO APPEAR TO..THE FACT THAT I LOOK 125 YEARS OLD HELPS ME TO GET INTO MY CHARACT-

CLICK!

AS FOR THE ROAST CHICKEN FLAVOUR, —LITERALLY AND METAPHORICALLY THE RESIDUE OF THOSE OFTEN ILLUSORY **SPECIAL OCCASIONS** WHEN A FOWL WOULD BE ROASTED...

I'LL COME BACK TO YOU ON THIS ONE.

...LEAVING BEHIND A **TASTY GREASE**, AS SATISFYING TO THEIR JUSTIFIABLY UNDISCRIMIN-ATING PALATES AS THE **FLESH** ITSELF!

SORRY TO INTRUDE, BUT I WAS FASCINATED BY YOUR THESIS...

...I MEAN, FOR ME, NOTWITHSTANDING THE OBVIOUS **ORAL GRATIFICATION** TO BE DERIVED FROM THE INSTANT AND REGULAR CONSUMPTION OF INEXPENSIVE MORSELS, AWAKENING LIBIDINOUS ANTICIPATION OF THE **WHOLE**, I.E. BAGS OF CHIPS, CHICKEN IN THE BASKET...

...SUCH FLAVOURS STIMULATE A REGRESSION TO **PRE-GENITAL PLEASURES** — WHAT KLEIN HAS TERMED THE **TOMATO SAUCE PHASE.**

BUT HOW DO YOU ACCOUNT FOR **PRAWN COCKTAIL** FLAVOUR... BASED ON THE MOST INSOLENT OF NOUVEAU-RICHE HORS D'OEUVRES AND 3 TIMES REMOVED FROM IT'S POLYNESIAN ORIGINS?

I ALWAYS THOUGHT IT CAME FROM NORWAY.

FAG ENDS

WELL SIR....... HAVE WE REACHED A DECISION?

BILL MARTIN

ER — THREE PACKETS OF PLAIN, PLEASE

SHALL WE SIT OVER HERE?

DO YOU GET MANY OF THEIR SORT IN HERE?

THEY COME HERE EVERY YEAR... STILL MAKES A CHANGE FROM PERSONAL COMPUTER REPS...

THIS LAGER TASTES LIKE PISS!

OF COURSE IT DOES.. — IT'S MEANT TO.. ITS VERY COLORATION IS SYNONYMOUS WITH THE **OUTBACK-** DEFINING ONE'S **TERRITORY**...MAN VERSUS NATURE...SUN, SAND AND THIRST.....

Coming Soon.. ||·|| FANTAISIE AU CACAO ||·||

featuring BARRY NORMAN

CONTINUING OUR ITALIAN NEO-REALISM SEASON ON VIDEO, HERE'S A DIFFICULT BUT REWARDING WORK...

M1 NORTH

EXPRESS NATIONAL

I WONDER IF MY OLD TREE-DEN IS STILL THERE?

THIS TIME I'LL *REALLY* MAKE THE EFFORT TO COMMUNICATE!

HI MOM...HEY, YOU SHOULDN'T HAVE GONE TO SO MUCH *TROUBLE!*

WELL—WE SEE YOU SO *RARELY!*

Reserved for OUR KID

...THERE I GO... IMMEDIATELY NEGATING THEIR DESIRE TO *GIVE!*

IN THE GARDEN...

...WHAT ELSE?—OH, MRS. WARDLE'S YOUNGEST IS GETTING MARRIED...YOU KNOW, SHE LOST HER HUSBAND.. THERE ARE SOME NEW PEOPLE IN NUMBER 42....

TEAS READY BOYS!

WISH I COULD DRUM UP SOME *ENTHUSIASM!*

AS SEEN ON NORMAN WISDOM

FASCINATING HOW LIFE SOMEHOW CARRIES ON...

WOULD YOU LIKE ANYTHING ELSE TO EAT?

COW PIE

I MUST RESIST THE COMPULSION TO TAKE *CONTROL!*

NO! STAY WHERE YOU ARE! I'LL PUT THE KETTLE ON.

LONG SILENCE, THEN...

♪DING♪ DONG!

AH—THAT'LL BE UNCLE REG AND AUNTIE VI.

DAILY EXPRESS
Reagan: My Hopes For Peace
Joan Collins

GOD! HOW CAN HE READ THAT JUNK?

SO... YOU'RE NOT *SPLICED* YET THEN, OUR ROGER? STILL, I DARE SAY YOU'VE GOT A *BIT O' STUFF* TUCKED AWAY DOWN IN THE SMOKE, EH?

HOW CAN I CHALLENGE HIS SEXIST ASSUMPTIONS?

KICK

NO—I HAVE MANY WOMEN FRIENDS, BUT NO-ONE IN PARTICULAR IN THE *PAIR-BONDING* SENSE.

WELL THANKS FOR A LOVELY TIME... SORRY ABOUT XMAS...OH, DIDN'T I TELL YOU? I'M SPENDING IT WITH SOME FRIENDS!

KIDS!..THEY GROW UP IN FRONT OF YOUR EYES!

BACK IN TOWN...

SO HOW WAS THE PRODIGAL VISIT?

OH YOU KNOW—THE USUAL GUILT ABOUT NOT MAKING ENOUGH EFFORT, MIXED WITH AN OEDIPAL DESIRE TO BE SUBMERGED IN CHEESE AND TOMATO SANDWICHES.

THE MAN WHO COULD NOT LAUGH

A **MODERN FOLK TALE** FROM THE COLLECTIVE UNCONSCIOUS OF THE **BROTHERS GRIMM,** PSYCHICALLY TRANSMITTED THROUGH THE MEDIUM OF MR. WOLFGANG AMADEUS SHAWCROSS (BELOW)

CANTEEN

WHAT'S UP, BAZ? YOU HAVEN'T TOUCHED YOUR **TUNA ROLLS.**

I DUNNO...I GUESS I'M FED UP WITH WORKING IN **CURRENT AFFAIRS**.. —ALL **DISPUTES, DISASTERS** AND **DEADLINES**...I NEED A CHANGE!

...I'M WORRIED ABOUT HIM, ROD,— HE'S GOING DOWNHILL FAST, HIS HEART'S NOT IN IT. COULD YOU HAVE A WORD WITH ANNA?

BRRR-BRRR! CLATTER-CLATTER -DING! -CLATTER

YES...THE WAY I SEE IT, ANNA, IT WOULD BE GOOD TO PUT BAZ IN CHARGE OF **COMEDY** —I MEAN, IF A GAG CAN MAKE **HIM** LAUGH, IT'LL MAKE **ANYONE** LAUGH!! —WHADDYA THINK?

SURE!..WE'RE THINKING OF RESHUFFLING OUR PRODUCTION STAFF ANYWAY...SEE IF WE CAN GET A BETTER **DARTS TEAM**— BOTTOM OF THE LEAGUE LAST YEAR...

AT THE NEXT PRODUCTION MEETING...

SO...WE'D LIKE ALAN TO MOVE OVER FROM RELIGIOUS AFFAIRS TO AGRICULTURE, JOAN, FROM AGRICULTURE TO EDUCATION, AND BAZ—YOU'LL **LOVE** THIS— YOU'RE TO TAKE ON **LIGHT ENTERTAINMENT**...HOW DOES THAT GRAB YOU?

BAZ

ANYONE WHO STILL SAYS '**HOW DOES THAT GRAB YOU**' IS DEFINITELY A **CAREER HAZARD.**

WELL, OF COURSE I'LL GIVE IT A GO.

WELL—HERE I AM! ...JUST THINK, THIS ROOM HAS SEEN 'EM **ALL**....TED RAY, AL READ, HANCOCK, BOB DANVERS--WALKER....

MIRTH DEPT.

TIME FOR YOUR SCRIPT CONFERENCE, BAZ.

O.K...SEND 'EM IN!

...THE SERIES IS BUILT AROUND THE LIVES AND LOVES OF 3 APARTMENT-SHARING **COMMUNITY ARCHITECTS**....

...WE FEEL THAT **SAUCY POSTCARD HUMOUR** IS SERIOUSLY UNDER-VALUED IN T.V. COMEDY. THE CARICATURES AND GROTESQUES WOULD BE SUFFICIENTLY DISTANCING TO AVERT CHARGES OF **SEXISM**...

WER-**HEY!!** -TOO RIGHT, REG!

...IT'S A SITCOM.... BASED ON MY OWN EXPERIENCE AS A SINGLE-PARENT SHEEPFARMER... **GERMAINE** INHERITS A COUNTRY ESTATE AND ATTEMPTS TO COMBINE **WRITING** WITH BEING A **MOTHER** AS WELL AS EXHIBITING **RARE BREEDS**..

YEAH!

HEY!

REALLY BORING...

SO PASSÉ.

...WE'D MAKE IT UP AS WE WENT ALONG..

...WRITE ALL OUR OWN MATERIAL

KINDA **ENID BLYTON** MEETS **LEN DEIGHTON**..

WE CAN HEAR THE **PLAUDITS** NOW..

..LOTSA AD LIBS...

RADICAL DIMENSION..

ZANY..

REAGAN..

THATCHER..

WHACKY...

AND-SIX MONTHS LATER ••••••

O.K. ANNA, I'LL CALL ANOTHER MEETING.

ROD? LISTEN-WE HAVE A PROBLEM. SINCE BAZ'S BEEN IN L.E. HE'S GOT RID OF **ALL COMEDY** FROM THIS CHANNEL!

WE NEED SOMEONE LESS **CYNICAL**, ROD, -LESS **CRITICAL**! DAMMIT—WE ALL NEED A GOOD **LAUGH** NOW AND AGAIN!

RATING CHART.

Boss of the Whole Shooting Match

..SO YOU SEE, BAZ - IN A WAY IT'S A STEP **BACKWARDS**, IN ANOTHER WAY IT'S A STEP **SIDEWAYS** - PERHAPS INTO A MORE APPROPRIATE FIELD...

MIND WHAT YOU'RE STEPPING IN, EH BAZ? ARF-ARF!

I THINK **RELIGIOUS AFFAIRS** COULD REPRESENT A FASCINATING CHALLENGE!

AND SO...

RIGHT... READY, FLOOR? -READY EVERYONE?... AND... **CUE TITLES**!

10...9....8... DAMN—MY WATCH HAS STOPPED.

OK...THE **CHURCH** IS AN EASY TARGET FOR COMEDY, YEAH?..ALL THAT BUNUEL STUFF, VICAR JOKES ETC..IT'S BECAUSE YOU'RE ALL SCARED STIFF!! AND WHAT YOU FEAR, YOU **BARE YOUR TEETH AT**!! FEAR-AND **HATRED**!. PULLING FACES, PULLING THE **TRIGGER**... FIRST SLIDE PLEASE...

COOL IT, PADRE, -REMEMBER.- THIS IS THE **FESTIVE SEASON**!

TAKE 2

OK! HAVE WE GOT A SHOW FOR YOU **TONITE**, LAZANGELMEN! PAUL DANIELS WILL BE ALONG LATER TO TURN **WATER** INTO **WINE**...(HE WORKS FOR ODDBINS ON THE SIDE-NO, JUST KIDDIN', FOLKS- AND FOR THE FIRST TIME ON T.V. I'LL BE RAISING FROM THE DEAD-**JIM REEVES, BUDDY HOLLY** AND **THE KING**!!

WILD APPLAUSE!

...A NATION IN TRANSIT...

COCOA SIR?

TICKETS PLEASE

PAWS IN COMFORT PETS HOTEL H.C. T.V. P.A.L. NO VACANCIES

WELL IF YOU-EVER PLAN-TO MOTOR WEST...

MUM-I FEEL SICK!

DID WE PACK THE PARTY ICE-BREAKERS?

WHATEVER YOU DO, DON'T MENTION THE NAME DEREK HATTON IN FRONT OF DAD-O.K?

AND THE FAMILY REUNION,

MAN IS BORN FREE BUT IS EVERYWHERE IN AFGHAN SLIPPER SOCKS.

WHY DO YOU KEEP GIVING US CLOCKWORK TOYS, UNCLE TIM-YOU SOME KIND OF FETISHIST?

-SIGH!-IT DOESN'T SEEM LIKE A YEAR SINCE LAST XMAS.

CAN I GO FOR A RIDE ON MY NEW C.S. TRIKE?

NO! YOUR DINNER'S ON THE TABLE.

AFTERSHAVE

Brand New Shirt

SPACE SHIP 1

£11.99 FROM LOCAL GARAGE.

DENIM

ELLO 'ELLO 'ELLO! – NOT INTERRUPTING ANYTHING WE HOPE!

THE ROYAL FAMILY SPENT THE DAY QUIETLY ATTENDING CHURCH AND DOING THE CROSSWORD.

BEFORE THE SLOW RETURN TO NORMALITY BEGINS.

OUR NEXT VIDEO SHOWS IN 11 SYMBOLIC EPISODES HOW A CHILD FOUND IN A DUSTBIN ADAPTS TO SOCIETY...

WELL, THAT WASN'T SO BAD...ALL OVER FOR ANOTHER YEAR

WHADDYA MEAN? WE'VE STILL GOT NEW YEAR'S EVE TO GET THROUGH!

Tulsa 24 hrs

NATIONAL

3 DAYS ON A CAMP BED! THINK I'LL PHONE THE OSTEOPATH TOMORROW.

COME ON EVERYONE – FORM A CIRCLE-IT'S ALMOST 12 O'CLOCK!

1987 IS GOING TO BE THE YEAR OF MY VIDEO NOVEL!

….. This juxtaposition of colour and texture also gives the clothes a chameleon-like quality, some ecclesiastical, some flamboyant, others simply chic….

NOW *HOLD ON!* WE SHOULDN'T ASSUME WE'RE DOING THIS IN *COSTUME!*.. I ENVISAGE WHITE BOILER SUITS, A BARE STAGE….

YES, BUT DEBBI,—THIS IS A *FAMILY SHOW*—PEOPLE WANT *CIRCUS* AS WELL AS *BREAD!* I'D GO FOR PLENTY OF SLAPSTICK!…*LOTSA* BIG PRODUCTION NUMBERS, AUDIENCE PARTICIPATION—THE WHOLE WORKS!

NO, DEBBI HAS A POINT, KRIS… WE'VE ONLY A CERTAIN AMOUNT OF MONEY TO PLAY AROUND WITH… I DON'T THINK WE CAN RUN TO A *FULL ORCHESTRA* THIS YEAR, FOR INSTANCE.. STILL, RAYMOND CAN DO A CRACKING JOB ON HIS *SYNTHESIZER* AND *RHYTHM BOX!*

IN THAT CASE, I MAY AS WELL LEAVE RIGHT NOW!

ME TOO!

JUDI—LISTEN… I *NEED* TO PLAY THE ARCHBISHOP'S REPRESENTATIVE—THE PART WAS *WRITTEN* FOR ME…. I CAN BRING *DEPTH* TO THE CHARACTER…

I'M NOT STAYING HERE TO BE INSULTED!

I'M SURE YOU CAN, TONI,—EVERYONE KNOWS YOU'RE THE *JACQUES COUSTEAU* OF INTERPRETATION… BUT I HAD YOU IN MIND FOR THE BACK END OF THE HORSE!

USE EVERY PART OF THE STAGE, LOVE… VERTICAL AS WELL AS HORIZONTAL SPACE…

IF IT'S ONE OF THOSE DO'S WHERE THE ACTORS HAVE TO LUG THEIR OWN SCENERY ABOUT, COUNT ME *OUT!* I'VE STILL GOT A HERNIA FROM DOING *FITZCARRALDO* LAST YEAR!

.THEN HARRY COMES ON WITH THE SNARE DRUM TO SYMBOLISE THE AWAKENING CONCIOUSNESS OF THE OPPRESSED MASSES!

THAT'S A LITTLE HEAVY ISN'T IT? —IT'S ONLY THE *THREE BEARS* FOR GODSAKE!

I'M OFF TO THE BAR… LET ME KNOW WHEN YOU'VE SORTED THIS OUT!

THE OPENING NIGHT

LADIES'N'GENTLEMEN, BOYS'N'GIRLS… DUE TO *UNFORSEEN CIRCUMSTANCES*, THIS YEAR'S PRODUCTION IS A LITTLE MORE TRUNCATED THAN USUAL….HERE WITH A VIRTUOSO *ONE-PERSON* INTERPRETATION OF 'DICK WHITTINGTON' IS YOURS TRULY…

CAT

…SO DICK SAYS TO THE DAME," DON'T PUT THE CAT IN THE WASHING MACHINE, GRANDMA—YOU'LL GET A SOCK IN THE PUSS…"

GROAN..

HEARD IT!

Sincerely yours,

BIFF

WRITTEN AND DRAWN BY *MICK KIDD* AND *CHRIS GARRATT*, FROM AN IDEA BY GODFREY BAZELY. ROSTRUM CAMERA KEN MORSE